Between Darkness & Trust

Between Darkness & Trust

LORRAINE FERRA

MoonPathPress

Poetry
ISBN
978-1-936657-37-7

Cover photo: by Deborah Trent

Author photo: by Judith Carlbom

Design: Tonya Namura using Latin Modern Roman &
Latin Modern Roman Dunhill

MoonPath Press is dedicated to publishing the finest poets
of the U.S. Pacific Northwest.

MoonPath Press
PO Box 445
Tillamook, OR 97141

MoonPathPress@gmail.com

http://MoonPathPress.com

for Deborah,
whose love is my guide
between darkness and trust

TABLE OF CONTENTS

III

Between Darkness & Trust

I

"Nothing is lost, but it can never be again as it was."

—*Loren Eiseley*

EVENING SKY
to my mother

Something this evening about
those whirls of light
strung out on the skyline
and the wing beats of birds
over the roof
pulls me back

to the clapboard house
and you pulling in sheets
that swell in the storm.
How you gathered
those armfuls of clouds
in through the kitchen
steamy with soup and promised

stories. Did I know then,
following your flight
from room to room,
that love is something always
passing? As now

a flush of swallows is filling
the window, and there goes
the sun, its last long
needle of light
sewing the house shut.

CARDINAL IN VERMONT

...the bird you thought you saw...had
absconded, leaving behind the emptiness
that hums a little in you now...
                                        —Robert Hass

Among my young mother's wishes
were two that I know never came true
through her forty-eight years:

to visit Vermont,

and to count a cardinal
in her sightings of birds.

Today, three-thousand miles from home,
and forty-four years after cancer pulled her
out of this life,

I sit near a gate in Bristol, Vermont
where that blood-red spirit lit
and sang out his heart to his mate
calling back from a shagbark hickory grove.

It seemed he was singing to me.

Then, like so many things
I've loved in my life,
staying too briefly to keep,

he flicked his wings and flew
radiantly out of my sight.

SCULPTURE

On the screened porch, sheltered
from the white-steel sun of August,

I watch a woman kneading
clay. Slowly her hands shape

the long curve of the throat,
the round, full breast, the wing.

Shadows of her fingers fall
across the bird, as if from dark

wings passing over the house.
I close my eyes and think of wind,

of water, of your long, slow passage,
of a swan slipping soundlessly

from the edge of a bank
into the cool cloister of cattails.

THIS WORLD

This world every day
finds a way to burden

my heart with its beauty
as this morning at five

dawn walked through the clouds
dragging the sash of your blue robe.

THE COST

Thinking of you leaving,
I think of the sun dissolving
to the light of the moon—

what we've gained,
what we've lost—
the cost of shining in the dark.

VILA CORTES DA SERRA, PORTUGAL

When he was a boy, my father says,
he went to sleep in the winter listening

to the livestock breathing under the floorboards,
the old house settling from the quarrels among

his father and uncles. He remembers them
in the mornings, leaving their beds long before light,

cursing their lives and the cattle, their frosted
breaths coiled under his window.

ON LEAVING YOUR HOMELAND
for my father

Almost sixty years
since you walked out of the hills of Gouveia,
left Vila Cortes da Serra for the last time,
running, not looking back, racing past
a grove of olives, your young mother watching
from a doorway of sun.

To the broken nets of New Bedford,
the asparagus fields of Roseville,
in the white dust of the flour mill—
it was not what you came for.
In the old world your mother wept
and wrote to your daughters:

Oh to be like a bird and fly over the ocean...

Today you celebrate the Feast of the Spirit—
smells of beef and mint rise everywhere.
Guitars play ancient fados, and a procession
begins at the door of the old church.
A child mounts the top step, unlatches a box
and sets free the white dove. You watch
as it flaps clumsily in new space then
soars toward the sun, dissolving, becoming
a dark form in the light behind your eyes.

FOR EVERY CHILD WHO IS GONE

Summer is going, the way
the sun just now clearing the porch

apportions the light and the darkness.
In her room my grandmother

drops the dark moons
of her beads, one

for every child who is gone.
I skip down to the street

where leaf shapes hang
like serpents from limbs.

Voices behind me fall,
winged pods drift on the wind.

Far-off lights blossom
into strange red flowers

as I chase my lengthening shadow
through the braided light of trees.

AUTUMN AGAIN

Night lifts above the bay,
slow as a great blue heron
folding the dark.

Someone lights a lamp at a window,
wood smoke moves toward me
from a black roof.

I see my grandmother waking,
opening the stones of her hands
to the morning. I hear the murmur

of litanies: Joao, Emilia, Eduardo—
names scattered like seeds
on the wind drift...

I turn to go in. Beside me the silver
birch leans down heavily,
brushing its limbs on the window.

EATING BREAD

to my grandmother

Your last day on earth,
Antonia Maria Batista,
and bread in the oven.

For eighty-one years
you fed your children,
your grandchildren,
your great grandchildren,
bargaining with the earth, the sky,
the few grains in your clenched hands.

Today you lie on the brass bed
in your flowered apron
your face and hair a white
flower on the pillow,
the smell of bread filling the room,
your words coming like shadows.

Take the bread out of the oven, you say.

A round shining loaf of bread
for your children.

ANOTHER COUNTRY
for my father

You fall asleep in a chair
in your grandchildren's house,
in your lap a story of a boy and a girl

following a trail of pebbles and bread
back to their home in the woods.
For now you are lost in the immense

swells of the sea that left you
wordless on a shore whose name
you never learned to pronounce.

For now you forget your first wife
gone for thirty years and the second
who sings to her shadow in a sterile room.

Water boils on the stove, steam
streams down the pane
like the rain that falls in your dream

of a boy herding his sheep toward
a darkening hillside. My sister
calls you to supper again and again.

Deep in your ear her voice trails
the wind climbing the hills
of another country.

WHAT IS KEPT

When I look again I find him
walking home before dusk

from the flour mill, white dust
on his boots, heading

to the garden behind the house,
looking for signs.

His knees in the soil,
he feels the corn silk, the kale leaves,

and shows me the green shoots.
Taking my hand

he goes in for his supper.
Fifty years, and another

winter lingers here, its stubble
bending into small pools of light.

All that's left turns back
to this man at the end of the day

entering the house through the kitchen,
the table spread with a clean white cloth.

SENESCENT

Pick the fig fallen to the lawn,
swollen, heart split open
to the heat, taste the bruised
meat of sweetness.

Listen for the psalms on the weathered
lips of bearded iris, in the lisp of wind,

for the pulse of sap rising
in the oldest maples.

Haven't the hours, worn as wind
in their slow roll of desire, brought you
a little riper to this moment?

Doesn't each ruckled leaf unlatched
from the branch still hold the sun
most lambent when going down?

And here is the dog, rearranging
the pain in her legs to follow you
once more out the door.

Believe in what is given, taken,
praise and grieve—

the rain barrel filled
and spilling
over.

AWAITING THE BIOPSY REPORT

All afternoon starlings knot
taut wires of telephone lines,

crosshatching the light,
raddling the barefoot sky.

I've been inside all day,
door locked, windows closed

against the cold, afraid
perhaps you'd come.

AFTER MAJOR SURGERY

Last week I watched
a late whimbrel lift

weightlessly over the water
from this stand of cattails

near the pond,
making flying seem

like nothing, something easy
in the curve and turn

of a life heading home.
There are no whimbrels

here today, only
a maverick sky

and the reeds
rising once again after the rain.

CRESCENT MOON

How happy to be home
from the hospital

under these swells of clouds
scudding above

our cedar-shake house
by the coast where

every day crows hold
bold parties in the yard,

and tonight the bay
becomes a living room

for the moon
who drops in, sporting

a new white sail.

FOG

Sometimes, to see
what's there, everything

must disappear, as now
fog moving over the marsh

taking trees, reeds,
sky only in water

growing smaller, as though
through a lens narrowing

to the blue heron
working the shoreline,

vanishing with each
slow step from

a world I've wanted
too much to hold.

POVERTY

To know, to see things
the way a window looks in
and out of itself,

as when you walk a long time down
the same road and meet yourself
in shadows of trees, birds, wind…

Yet something as familiar as light
turns from your eyes
and is gone.

You stand in a darkening field
your feet planted
like heavy stones in the earth.

IN THE THROATS OF BIRDS

Something gray and brooding
peers into your room

interrupting the end of a dream.
You pull up the shade

and think you've caught
whatever it was

sharpening its knives
on the tips of the hills.

Then you walk down the hall
to put on the coffee

and it's there—
morning—

in the throats of birds
guarding their nests,

pouring an old song
into your cup.

KITE

I attach my heart
to a roll of twine

and let it loose
over the bay.

How easy,
I think,

watching it
floating away

light as a leaf
through the clouds,

fluttering back
when I spool it in.

DECIDUOUS

Before I die, I'd like
to learn how to change

the clothes of my life
simply

by standing still
rooted

year after year
in whatever weather

brings these trees—
sycamore, maple, ash—

again to this gold
extravagance, leaving us

feeling at once rich
and wordless.

II

"When I am among the trees...
I would almost say that they save me, and daily."

—*Mary Oliver*

TALKING TO TREES

Rifle stocks are carved
from you, crossbeams
in the cabin's walls,
a violin and bow that

together praise Mozart.
Dogwood, yew, new alder,

first burst at field's edge,
snags of birch, masts

of madrone tossed up
in the sea foam.

Pencils shaped from cedar,
paper formed from pine,

page after page filling
with words better sung

by your needles in wind,
your rippling tongues.

NAMES OF TREES

Adverbs of wind

Red flashes of passion
in autumn

At daybreak
widening corridors
of sun-spill

Darkening cathedrals

Congregations of owls
worshipping moons
in small eyes

In storms
green genuflections
glissandos
Gregorian chants

Black sentences
in the dusk
we still can't read

AFTER PASSING A REVIVAL TENT

I walk down to the woods
to listen to the creek talk,
to the water resounding its hymns

over the smooth tongues of stones;
and I remember Sundays
in church as a child,

the long morning of my life before me,
I sat under the microphoned
drone of sermons

while the sun spoke its parables
behind the stained glass
of a different world;

and my thoughts drifted with it
as they do now, following its spill
down the lichened trunks of the trees

into the creek. All around me
this morning everything is doing
what it must do—

the snake sliding back
into the uncertain shadows of ferns,
the jays cracking open the air

in the ongoing arguments of birds,
the butterfly folding
and unfolding

in the easy breeze and lull
of a birch leaf coming down.
I cup my hands into the moving

clarity of this cold creek
forever going back to the sea,
and I know, no matter

where I go in this world
of leaf-float and mud-slide,
I am continually being saved.

FINDING THE POEM

Night comes. Trees fall
asleep in their black feathers.

I reach up to cup the half-
moon's light. One star

flickers on, brightens
in the breathing silence…

INVOCATION AT DAYBREAK

Blue knife in the eastern sky, paring the night
into pieces of light, illumine this page.

First finch calling out unseen in nearby tree,
awaken the sleeping notes at the base of my throat.

Litany of leaves, supplicant chant of the breeze,
be sacrament of words drawing clarity to the day.

Blind and deaf dog curled up at my feet,
(quiet barks like hiccups in half-sleep),

teach me the language between darkness and trust
and what the silence might say.

LIGHT

My blind friend tries
to tell me what light is.

She remembers sleeping
on a screened porch in summer,
hearing the first blue jays
swelling the jack pine.

It has something to do,
she says, with
awakening.

DAILY

Breathe it in—

the day coming on
stoop-shouldered

in this hour's torn
jacket of light.

What's left
of yesterday's work

waits on the desk
like grass under snow.

A junco claims the first
word of the day—

a tentative trill
in the bush.

Time to open the door
to my own small

room in the world.
No matter.

Where else
would I want to be,

turning on the warmth
of the writing lamp,

beginning again
where I left off,

breathing it in.

DOING NOTHING

We must learn how to waste time conscientiously...
—Suzuki Roshi

Writing of the contemplative life, Thomas Merton
shares the Zen master's advice, then adds:
to feel free to do nothing, without feeling guilty.

All morning I learn, spending hours with lines
leading at times nowhere in particular. I am
as happy and lost as the child outside

steering his toy trucks over the infinite collapsible
bridges a child's play often is, all the while
singing a mind-wandering tale to his imagined friend.

ARS POETICA: OUR BLIND &
DEAF DOG KNOWS

that every bush holds the hush of some presence
brushed again past stone or stick or fence;

that any gust can give off whiffs of squirrel, rabbit, deer,
mixed in the sudden rush ruffling her hair;

that sniffing her way through the day turns up
news of random, transient things waiting everywhere.

POEM WRITTEN IN HURN'S FIELD
AFTER A CLASS

Next time my students ask
what a poem means,

I'll tell them: Let it be
the snowmelt

at the mouth of the meadow
where the bull elk comes

to drink at daybreak.
Read it the way

the elk drinks from the pool,
doesn't gaze into it.

Let it be neither you
nor the elk,

but that difference.
As you read, know

that the pool is
a different pool

when you drink from it
again. And when you cup

your hands into the poem,
let it be your hands,

and the cold,
and the elk

retreating
into shadows.

Let it be what is
and isn't there.

And let it be your eyes
in the eye of the pool

brimming now
with the light

of stones
           and stars.

WHEN ASKED HOW POETS
MAKE A LIVING

It depends on the poet, I say
to the tenth-grade boy slumped
at his desk by the window,

then mention readings
and teaching classes like this
as ways some poets get by.

But beyond the brim of his Budweiser
cap, I catch the tall tree line of pines
ancient and clear as words

against snow, afternoon sun
pausing over everything brighter
than ever before.

GREAT BLUE HERON AT
HASTINGS POND

Every morning he's here and you come,
past poplars and scotch broom,
through bur-reeds and bog willows,

to find him fishing the shallows
of the opposite shore.

To catch that quickness of eye and beak,
the harmony of hunger and skill, until

he lifts, his wings sculling the air
toward a harbor of firs.

Each morning you come
to feel that pulse of the pond
and wait for that wing beat, for

your own rising into the day.

BIRD NOTES
for Deb, who loves birds,
a note a day during her birthday week

All afternoon gusts of robins
plunder the pyracantha berry bushes
then stagger up the sidewalk,
drunk, and full-bellied.

*

Breeze-ruffled feather from
the marsh wren's chest,
stuck to the cusp of a broken shell.

*

A crow, so
sure of himself,
parks on a no-parking sign.

*

The calling back and forth of two
song sparrows in morning dark.
The four notes, the trill, then silence…
then answer. Our bodies stir
to this song through the window
and then to a song of our own.

*

From a long sentence of snow geese, one
black-tipped wing feather floating down to the pond.

*

Dead grebe, storm-tossed into a hollowed dune,
long beak still piercing a scaled dried skin—
all he knew of hunger and hope in that wind.

*

Music in the yard—
house finch, oh to sing like you,
mellow piccolo!

WAKINGS

Dawn, and the curve
of your hip shadowed
on the wall.

Eyelashes rising, falling,
slow and soft as a moth's
wings before flight.

If only
it could always
be this way—

each morning your steady
breathing beside me,
while outside

an orchestra of song
birds, fluttering,
tuning up in the trees.

DESIRE

knocks at the door
just before breakfast.

She rode a boxcar, she says,
all the way from the coast

and proceeds to butter
the toast I set on the table.

She promises to leave
as soon as she's eaten,

but do I have some preserves,
and maybe an egg or two,

and a cup of coffee
sweetened with cream?

SUNDAY EVENING, DEEP SUMMER

The weekend is over, the guests gone,
night coming on, like a blessing.

The sky opens its breviary of stars.
Listen: the kyrie of a horse's neigh

from the pasture, a breeze
nickering through the trees, now

crickets chanting in the slow
kingdoms of grass.

POET AT THE END OF SUMMER

Purple finch,
with your wine-streaked
chest and liquid song,
feasting beneath
dandelion moons,
filling your belly
with mayflies
and thimbleberries,
would you
look for a job
today
if you were in
my shoes?

THE COMFORTS OF
ANIMAL FIDELITIES

Walking the salmonberry
path through the woods,
we stop for the deer, a pair

of black-tailed yearlings
stilled by our sudden
entrance and sound. We stand

still in the bell-clear air,
in the stillness of deer, and liquid
clarity of incredulous eyes.

Two song sparrows unseen
in the tangled tops of the trees
sweeten the air between them.

We speak low and close
in the ferns, of love
and animal loyalty.

The deer slacken their stance,
unlock their eyes from ours,
and bend down to browse

in the bracken, the slender one
nuzzling the other's ear. We watch
as they turn and move on

through the red morning light
of madrone. Other worlds. Yet
there are these small distances,

these comforts of animal fidelities.

SNOWSHOE HARE

To move through the world
unnoticed, to be

the snow and not the snow
is the secret, some say, of keeping

the cold at bay.
He is turning now in the early

dusk of mid October,
a furred patch by the birch bark,

a mottled flash in the foxglove.
I listen for him here

in these near-winter woods
where wind plays a sleight-of-hand

in the switchgrass, and believe
there is in each of us

a temporary shield of concealment,
a magician's hat,

where something is always changing
until changing finally into itself.

NOBODY'S CROW

He drops from the top
of the cracked Douglas-fir,

a black, scratchy
vowel on the fence.

His rowdy insistence
shatters the sky behind him.

An airborne hobo,
he thrives on the vagaries

of wind. *Caw, Caw.*
Let your life be

a raucous *Yes.* A full-
throated *No.*

CRAVINGS

November sun backing up
behind clouds. I have

a craving for colors,
for what's hidden beyond

blue and grey. Off
to the woods to see what's

left: red bark of madrone,
grosbeak in snowberries,

gold leaves from the vine maple
piling up among firs,

purple finch and juncos
perched on a pine.

What else? American goldfinch,
yellow shine of a Coors can

in rainwater, rufous-sided towhee,
then rain again promising

to come down hard. Something
slowing in the bracken,

something like autumn, tired
of the long shift, of tracking

its life through the trees,
tired of grieving.

NOVEMBER

Fall's broken fence
propped and fixed
back to the post.

The last windfall apples
cooked and stored
for winter.

Our lives pared down
to these offerings
of sweetness and wind.

Beyond madrone & hawthorn,
rain-sleek and smooth
as a bone,

two black brant geese
dive for the closing
eye of the pond.

Everything dark, wet,
shining, everything saying
Home.

ORCHARD

Because it is dusk and December,
orange trees are turning
black against the sky. A rutted bark

catches some last gold. A light
goes on in a distant window. The scrub jays
that live in the lodge pole behind the barn

have settled their quarrels for the day.
I walk back to the house, leaving
oranges on the cold ground.

WINTER SOLSTICE

Again, sudden and thin
as a quick slip of sun,

as the last lip of light
on the rim of your cup,

the kind darkness of hands
blessing your life as it is.

Whatever needs to be done
falls asleep in the trees,

goes down with the creek
sounding the constancy of work

done well and still here
year after unfailing year.

WAKING TO SNOW

Once every year
an old drifter
walks into town
while we sleep.
In a frayed pocket
he carries a dream,
luminous
as a new key,
lighter than
a small coin.

Before dawn
he takes it out
and turns it
in the locks
of drowsiness,
tucks it under
a feathered pillow
then taps at the door
and leaves,
his long white beard
trailing behind.

FALLING LIGHT

Evening and new snow
falling in the yard.

The cat sits motionless
at the window, a white star

on her chest, the moon
glazing the hump of her back.

She waits for the waxwings
that plundered the crab apple

heavy now with falling light,
its few silver tongues

hanging in the cold air.
Watching, I know

there are things that fall
wordlessly as the weariness

of this December day,
or the way dusk leans

over my shoulder, a reparation
as it turns toward the night.

The cat sleeps. Snow falls
and falls through my face

in the glass. I lose my eyes
in a thicket of small wet flakes.

JANUARY

It is always the snow,
the unplowed road to the house,

the mailbox nailed to the porch
white and empty.

Down the hill the neighbor
is spinning his tires on ice,

rushing to enter the traffic
this weather has brought to a halt.

I have come to trust
the incredible: all of this falling

toward earth, meltwater
running the eaves in spring,

the iridescence of dusk, ice, starling.
Tomorrow I'm fifty-one.

It has taken this long
to begin learning the language of snow.

To land like an unwritten page.
To say nothing.

AVALANCHE
for Sandra at Honeycomb Cliffs

Spring, and we stop by a stream
where pines rise through the clouds.

On the slopes timber broken by winter
cooks in the sun—old slow barges

hauled up from the sea. You point north
to the saddle that held the snow's secret

for months, and the place maps a journey
you've made more than once: back to

the three-story house rattling in winter,
your father and mother drunk and smoking

in bed, and you, thirteen again, sitting out
the night, the night feeling its way along walls.

On the trail ahead, an aspen pulled up
by the slide, sprouts a new shoot from its roots,

a young leaf trembling in wind. You kneel,
breathe-in the new growth, and move on.

VERNAL EQUINOX

March turning over, and winter
hanging its coat on the fence.

Last year's leaves, white shoots
on the dogwood, the agreement

of subject and verb,
of past and present tense.

Under the eaves the spider
returns to its center

on silk guylines of light.
I'm here by the window

with my notebook and pen,
climbing back into my life

one spare line at a time.

III

"How shall we hold on, when everything bright
falls away?"

—*Charles Wright*

FLYWAY

watching geese in the weeks following September 11

In a fever of wings
the first geese
abandon the ponds,

every morning
flying low and honking
over the house,

an invasion of wing beats
making my heart rush
and the leaves

of every tree and bush
shiver and ripple
under the slapping

waves of wings. For days
acres of sky
blacken with birds

as the toll of lives rises
from steel wings
flying in a different

darkness. Today,
headlines aside,
coffee cooling in my cup,

I'm drawn again
in this thin, pre-dawn
light, to these birds,

these ambassadors of air,
following no doctrines
but the directions of wind,

no tenets of infallible
truths, only a flyway
toward sun. And now

look—the sun is seeping
into the sky
through the clouds,

onto the wings of birds
bearing it once more
over this world.

Another
day, another
chance to change.

READING TU FU AT SUNSET
AFTER 9/11

All afternoon I've been alone
on the bank of the pond
reading aloud the heartbreaking
poems of Tu Fu. A drake drifts
near now and then as if to listen.
A breeze through cattails carries
winged pods across the water.
I lean back in the grass and watch
one cloud coming home
through a bleeding sky, an old poet
bearing the day's wounds on his back.

EVENING, POINT OF ARCHES

The sky darkens. Gulls
gather along the sea walls.

Starfish, washed ashore in the morning
tide, are home again in the sea. Far out,

gray whales follow long hollow
notes in the darkness. What do we know?

LISTENING TO ANIMALS

After a troubled day
I lie back and stroke
the sleeping cat
on my chest. She breathes
in, breathes out.

Her breathing sings
a psalm about
the toppling of kingdoms,
about the little armies falling
in the blades of the grass.

I breathe in,
breathe out, and feel
I could stand very still
in the midst of it all...

They say that Francis of Assisi,
lost on a journey
through a forest,
followed the song of a thrush

from tree to tree
until the bird finally
whistled him home.

SHOPPING

When the president was asked
after September 11, for advice on living
with the threat of terror, he said,

"Hug your kids and go shopping,"
words supposedly meant to provide comfort
and promote commerce.

Childless, I walked through the week,
shopped around and found

fall, and the far-off call of the mill whistle
hauling the day uphill;

poppies unclenching their golden fists
in morning sun;

the snail's silver trace across the porch;

clouds whose journeys have nothing to do with
arrival;

sword fern surrendering its blades under hemlocks;

absolution of sun just before dusk;

trust.

*

This morning, a kinglet, trusting the kingdom of air,
crashed into the just-washed window, proving
what seems clear can kill in a kingdom of lies.

And the morning news with its menus
of grief, tells us the stock market is up,
the economy on the rise...

I take a walk. I shop around.

7:00 A.M. POSTCARD FROM UTAH

Driving down I-15 with
the radio on—more lives lost

in roadside bombings,
and seabirds struggling

in oil-slick waters.
The sun just now hikes up

the Wasatch, and a magpie
carries his own news

to a telephone wire still heavy
with yesterday's snow. I miss

the blue skies of your eyes
in the mornings, the language

of those eyes translating
the only news I want to know.

COMPLINE, TRAPPIST ABBEY
Huntsville, Utah

Wind swallows the voices of the brothers
chanting psalms to the night
behind amber-lit windows.

Aspens on the hill howl and flail,
rearing their heads and wailing
against winter's wall of moonlight.

MONUMENT

Driving past Price Canyon, I enter
coal country, smokestacks
puffing like trains,
dark shale peeling the hills,
leftover snow black
on the roadside.

On Main Street in Helper, Utah,
dwarfing the Catholic church
where the painted arms of Jesus & Mary
welcome the dusk,
Big John, the coal miner,
swings a pickax over his shoulder.

He smiles and steps west
toward Spring Canyon
where twenty years ago
a town disappeared
in a shaft.

Starlings fall from his cap,
children run through his legs, brushing
the quiet snowfall of dust
off his boots.

THROUGH THE WINDOW
for Deborah

Some days the world feels
fierce, as now, dark

clouds charging headlong
toward a bigger storm

beyond this frame.
The day is lightning,

whitecaps, the tips
of sails dipping

in the bay, the nearing
combat of thunder and rain.

Below the window
in your flowered canvas

hat, you pull the last
of winter's weeds and pat

the mulch gently
around our young

rough-barked maple.
You plant a calm, steady

trust in a world
too uncertain without you.

GRATITUDE

For the single gold Ginkgo leaf
brought to the porch by the wind

and the way outgoing tides leave
a treasure now and then in the sand,

like a line I find in a first grader's poem:
I am as quiet as a pencil searching for a word.

Or knowing that with you I become
more than I am, as a tree changes with
birds or wind or a woman reading in its shade.

For that unexpected moment of pure eccentric
joy, wanting to throw open every shuttered
window down the street.

For the syntax of the hours, like language
pushing us away or pulling us close,

as this morning, waking to a world of political
lies, other than holding one another, how else
do we know trust and possibility?

5:00 A.M., BEAVER VALLEY ROAD

Curls of cattle's breath rise
above dark backs huddled
in the field beyond this fence

The moon loosens
her robes of night
and the sun shivers in tall grass

I drive into this lengthening
light, the sky spreading
a new blue sheet

ACKNOWLEDGEMENTS

Thanks to the editors and publishers of the following, where some of these poems, sometimes in slightly different versions, have appeared: *Bellowing Ark, CAB (Conversations Across Borders), Country Journal, Fingerlings, Free Lunch: A Poetry Miscellany, Iris: A Journal About Women, Mickle Street Review, Poet & Critic, Poets & Artists 1990 Calendar* (Bainbridge Island Arts Council), *Quarterly West, The Duckabush Journal, The Florida Review, The Seattle Times,* and *Westigan Review of Poetry.* "Autumn Again" and "Nobody's Crow" were letterpress printed as broadsides in limited editions of 100 copies by Canticle Press, Port Townsend, WA.

Previous chapbook collections which contained several of these poems: *Eating Bread* (Kuhn Spit Press, Port Townsend, 1994) and *What The Silence Might Say* (One-Crow-Dancing Books, Port Townsend, 2012).

The epigraph to part 1 is by Loren Eiseley in *All The Strange Hours* (Charles Scribner's Sons, 1975). The lines to part 2 are from Mary Oliver's poem, "When I Am Among the Trees" in *Thirst* (Beacon Press, 2006). The lines to part 3 are from Charles Wright's poem, "A Journal of the Year of the Ox" in *The World of the Ten Thousand Things* (Farrar Straus Giroux, 1990). The quote in "Cardinal In Vermont" is from Robert Haas's poem, "Mouth Slightly Open" in *Time And Materials* (The Ecco Press, 2007). The quotes in "Doing Nothing" are excerpted from David Steindl-Rast's essay in *Monastic Studies #10,* 1974.

Poems in Skagit River Poetry anthologies: "Nobody's Crow" *This Should Be Enough* (2002), "Evening Sky" *The Sound Close In* (2004), "Daily" *The Moment Witnessed* (2008), "Deciduous" *Into The Open* (2010), "Senescent"

Drawn To The Light (2012) and "Through The Window" *At The Water's Edge* (2014). "What Is Kept" was produced as a broadside (2016).

With gratitude to these first readers for their comments and suggestions on certain poems: M. L. Bean, Neal Bowers, Sally Green, Samuel Green, Kathryn Hunt, Leslie Kelen, Robert Mezey, Ron Offen, Richard Schramm, Don Stap, and Deborah Trent.

A depth of gratitude to my editor and publisher, Lana Hechtman Ayers, for her profound kindness and patience throughout the development of this publication.

Within these poems is the mentorship of my beloved mother, who died of cancer when I was a teenager. Early on she instilled my love of reading and writing by taking me weekly to our Carnegie Library, and buying my first writing desk when I was seven years old. Her presence is inherent throughout this collection.

ABOUT THE AUTHOR

Lorraine Ferra was born and raised in Vallejo, California, a seaport on the east side of the San Francisco Bay. She was a nun for seven years in a community in Fremont, California, where she majored in theology and education and taught in elementary and secondary schools.

After leaving the convent, she lived for several years in Salt Lake City, pursuing seminars in modern and contemporary poetry and creative writing under the directorship of Robert Mezey at the University of Utah.

Her poems have appeared in many literary journals and anthologies since 1976, and some are collected in *Eating Bread* (Kuhn Spit Press, 1994) and *What The Silence Might Say* (One-Crow-Dancing Books, 2012).

Her creative writing book, *A Crow Doesn't Need A Shadow: A Guide To Writing Poetry From Nature* (Peregrine Smith Books, 1994) has been endorsed by the National Council of Teachers of English.

Ferra is a recipient of a Utah Arts Council Award in Poetry and a Westigan Poetry Award selected by John Haines.

She has worked extensively for many years as a poet-in-residence with various state arts programs across the country and, since 2002, through the Skagit River Poetry Foundation in La Conner, WA.

Lorraine and her spouse, Deborah Trent, have lived for twenty-three years in Port Townsend, WA.